For:

Chris, Loretta, Diane, MaryAnn, Joanna, Celia, Ruth, Ellen, Judy, Shiya, and Kelly

— With love and gratitude for your amazing gifts and support

Mystical Manifestation
3rd edition
© April 2014 Rebecca Cohen

Table of Contents

Introduction

Mystical Manifestation, a self-help manifestation protocol, is both <u>grounded</u> in that it gives you specific steps to perform to create your heart's desires, and provides insight into why we get stuck; and <u>mystical</u> in that the energy accelerating the affirmations into reality comes from a mysterious, other-worldly place. **Mystical Manifestation** is presented herein in two parts:

1) **Divine Magic**, a manifestation technique – Divine Magic is comprised of creating affirmations, discovering the personal shift required in order for the affirmation to manifest, and creating an energy shift, utilizing a wand, specified motions, and symbols to break patterns that no longer serve us. Divine Magic works because it gives us the courage to embrace our authentic self, which enables us to manifest our heart's desires. Divine Magic aligns our mind with our heart and soul, which is the magic behind ascension, unstoppability, and manifestation.

2) **Mystic Transformation** – Mystic Transformation lists negative circumstances and the associated spiritual state that requires opening in order to release the circumstance. When this list is used as affirmations within Divine Magic, it creates a radical transformation to our state of grace arising from the absence of fear, so that we experience only joy from our heartfelt passions and pleasures.

Mystical Manifestation is part of **The Path to Heal**, a healing system that I developed over the last four years to help my clients rise above struggle. Much like **Mystical Manifestation**, the rest of the **Path** uses specific protocols to help locate the root of why we are sick or stuck, provides insight into this root, helps us discover the personal shift required to rise above struggle, and then raises our vibration to that of pure love and light using crystals, tunings forks, and natural essences. Full **Path** sessions are performed by trained **Path** practitioners only.

In developing **Mystical Manifestation** and **The Path to Heal**, I received insight through meditation and muscle testing, and then incorporated these insights into my client sessions. Over time, I came to realize that I was channeling the Egyptian goddess Isis through my development process. Because "Isis" also means "is is", these protocols come from All That Is.

This book provides step-by-step instruction on how to perform Divine Magic and how to incorporate Mystic Transformation into Divine Magic. The same material is also taught in a half-day class, information about which can be found at http://www.ThePathToHeal.com/training. Additionally, demonstrations of Divine Magic and muscle testing are available at www.ThePathToHeal.com on the Mystical Manifestation tab.

Divine Magic is a manifestation technique comprised of creating affirmations, discovering the personal shift required in order for the affirmation to manifest, and creating an energy shift, utilizing a wand, specified motions, and symbols to break patterns that no longer serve us. Divine Magic works because it gives us the courage to embrace our authentic self, which enables us to manifest our heart's desires. Divine Magic aligns our mind with our heart and soul, which is the magic behind ascension, unstoppability, and manifestation.[1] To perform Divine Magic, the following is required:

1) Rose quartz spiral wand – This wand provides a continuous loop of unconditional love and light resonating our hearts to our mind so that we can manifest our soul's purpose. It can be created simply by holding a long screw (for the spiral) and a piece of rose quartz in one's hand while doing the techniques. Or you can purchase a wand as long as it's spiral shaped and contains rose quartz. It can also be purchased on www.ThePathToHeal.com. If you already have a wand, do not use it unless it's a rose quartz spiral wand, as without these properties, the healing energy will be reduced.

2) Divine Magic Worksheet – This worksheet is found in this book and can also be printed from www.ThePathToHeal.com (Download section). Affirmations are written on this worksheet because it contains symbols that enhance the power of the affirmations.

3) The ability to dowse – Dowsing is a form of asking yes-or-no questions energetically to the universe (including your own inner truths and connectivity to the Divine). The two most common forms of dowsing are muscle testing and using a pendulum. See the Teaching Yourself to Dowse section of this book for more information.

4) Divine Magic technique instructions – found in this book.

Note: If you are significantly blocked on an issue, a complete **The Path to Heal** session would be very helpful to accelerate healing and manifestation.

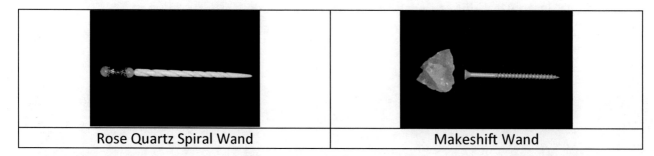

| Rose Quartz Spiral Wand | Makeshift Wand |

---

[1] Divine Magic also opens all of **The Path to Heal's** crystal grids for accelerated healing. These grids have been created by **Path** practitioners by placing crystals in a specific formation over a diagram.

Creating Your Affirmations

- Use the attached worksheet to write down your affirmations (can also be found on the Homepage of www.thepathtoheal.com under Downloads, and can be printed in black and white, or color). This worksheet must be used because the symbols at the top of the worksheet contain energy that raises your vibration to that of pure light, thereby aiding the manifestation process.

- Affirmations always begin with "I create".

- Affirmations should always include positive words. For example, it will be much more helpful for to you to write, "I create a fulfilling and rewarding job" rather than "I create a job that I no longer hate."

- If you are open to the outcome and trust the universe to bring what's best for you, keep the affirmations non-specific. For example, you can write, "I create the job of my dreams" rather than "I create a promotion next week to my boss's position."

- However, it is okay to write, "I create a promotion next week to my boss's position" if you specifically know what it is that will make you happy. While requesting a particular timeframe makes it harder for the universe to provide what you are asking for, asking for it can do no harm.

- You can create manifestations for others and perform them during Divine Magic. For example, you can write, "I create my husband having a loving and peaceful relationship with his mother."

- Because all manifestations through Divine Magic will occur only if the affirmations come from your heart, if an affirmation is not aligned with your heart, it simply will not manifest through this process.

- Affirmations to include in Divine Magic also come from the Mystic Transformation list discussed in detail later in this book

I create:

_____

_____

_____

_____

_____

_____

_____

_____

_____

_____

_____

_____

_____

_____

_____

_____

_____

_____

_____

_____

Name: _____ **Date:** _____

Divine Magic Instructions

1. Write a list of affirmations on the Divine Magic Worksheet.
2. Say the sentence below aloud. Fill in the blank with the first affirmation on your list.
3. Dowse to determine which sentence ending best fits (boxes below #1-12). If more information is needed as to the meaning of the sentence ending, you can ask yes / no questions while dowsing to receive details.
4. Perform the technique corresponding with the sentence ending with your spiral wand. Techniques are described in detail on the following pages.
5. Dowse to determine if there are additional sentence endings. If there are, repeat Step 4 with additional endings.
6. Move on to the next affirmation, repeating steps 2-5.
7. Repeat daily, adding and removing affirmations as desired. Sentence endings can change, so make sure you perform all steps each time you do an affirmation.

∞ *I create _____ from my heart by honoring my divine, authentic and blissful self by:*

Sentence endings:

calling someone's bluff 1	✳	standing up to a bully 7	✳
climbing any mountain 2	◎◎	standing up for what I know to be true 8	♾
forgiving _____ 3	2-6 ∞	taking charge of a situation 9	7 ∞
knowing myself 4	7-3	telling others what I need 10	1 ∞
promoting myself 5	7-2	transcending fear 11	7-1
seeing the solution (consciousness of truth) 6	6 ∞	unconditionally giving and receiving love 12	4 ∞

Sentence Ending Further Instruction

After dowsing a sentence ending, reflect on that ending. For example, if forgiving _____ comes up, ask yourself, who do I need to forgive? If taking charge of a situation comes up, ask yourself, what situation do I need to take charge of? You can also dowse while asking yes / no questions to get more information on all sentence endings. Feel free to add affirmations to help subsequent steps flow with ease. For example, if taking charge of a situation means discussing your desire to change jobs with your spouse, add an affirmation stating, "I create an easy, positive conversation with my spouse on my job switch."

If you get a "no" to all sentence endings, it may mean one of a few things:
   a. This affirmation isn't necessary to do today, as the manifestation energy is already working.
   b. Further healing is needed, such as a full **The Path to Heal** session.

Details On Techniques

The following pages contain diagrams to help you perform the techniques associated with each sentence ending. These techniques transmute energy, allowing us to break patterns that no longer serve us. Each technique and associated symbol has a corresponding energetic meaning that can be found in the symbol guide in the back of this book.

- The blue numbers in the boxes on the previous page correspond to the blue numbers on the following pages to guide you to the correct technique to perform.

- Once you locate the correct technique, point the wand at the figure on the page and trace the blue symbol (a few inches off the page).

- Alternatively, you can perform the same technique on yourself or on a client: Point the wand at yourself or the client while performing the technique.

- The black numbers over the symbols represent which chakras you will be performing the technique over. If you perform the technique by tracing the blue symbol on the page, you are already aligned with the right chakras (a chakra diagram is found on the inside back cover of this book).

- Most techniques are repeated three times. There are directions to the right of each figure specifying how many times to perform the technique.

- All techniques are to be performed quickly (which moves energy quickly). Performing the technique quickly is far more important than is attempting perfection.

- Once you become familiar with the techniques, you no longer need to refer to the diagrams on the following pages.

Technique Diagrams

calling someone's bluff 1		standing up to a bully 7	
	Name: Inifinity Flower 3 infinities forming flower over heart Perform 1x		Name: Sumbli-mation 3 infinities forming flower over heart, then 3 spins over heart, then spiral outwards
climbing any mountain 2		standing up for what I know to be true 8	
	Name: Eyes Into Soul Spiral right eye, then S-curve, then spiral left eye		Name: Spinal Adjustment Linked infinitiies from base of spine to top of head

Technique Diagrams

Forgiving _____ 3	**2-6** ∞ 3 inifinities from 2nd chakra to 6th chakra	taking charge of situation 9	**7** ∞ 3 inifinities over 7th chakra
knowing myself 4	**7-3** Spin 3x from 7th chakra to 3rd chakra	telling others what I need 10	**1** ∞ 3 inifinities over 1st chakra

Technique Diagrams

promoting myself 5	**7-2**	transcending fear 11	**7-1**
	Spin 3x from 7th chakra to 2nd chakra		Spin 3x from 7th chakra to 1st chakra
seeing the solution (consciousness of truth) 6	∞ 6	unconditionally giving and receiving love 12	∞ 4
	3 infinities over 6th chakra		3 infinities over 4th chakra

Teaching Yourself to Dowse

Muscle testing: the easiest form of dowsing to use while doing Divine Magic

- Make a ring on each had with your thumb and index finger. Then link these two rings together.
- Create a little tension between the two rings. Set the intention that you will receive a "yes" answer when your hands separate with ease, and a "no" answer when you feel some tension between your two hands.
- Ask a simple yes/no question that you know the answer to, such as: "Is my name Rebecca"?
- After asking, pull your fingers apart and see if your hands separate with ease, or whether you feel tension and your hands remain linked.
- Ask multiple yes/no questions until you can feel the difference between a yes and a no.
- When muscle testing to perform Divine Magic, there are absolute rules for success:
  a. Always go with your first "yes"; don't double check. If you double check, you'll likely get a different answer, as you've created doubt.
  b. The first yes is always correct.
  c. If muscle testing doesn't come easily, fake it until you make it: your faking it is your inner voice giving you the right answers anyway!

There are many forms of muscle testing not described here. Feel free to use any method that works for you.

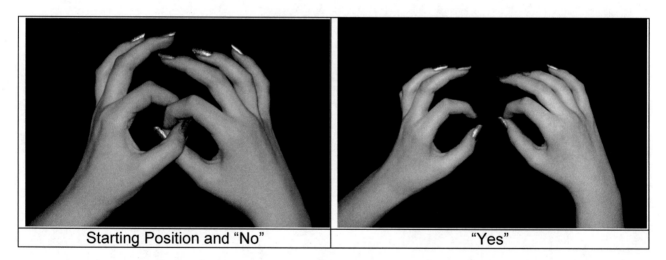

| Starting Position and "No" | "Yes" |

Pendulum: more difficult to use for Divine Magic as it takes longer to get yes/no answers

- You can use any pendulum that you own or decide to purchase.
- Set the intention that the pendulum swings clockwise for a yes, and counterclockwise for a no.
- Ask questions as suggested above to practice using your pendulum.
- If you already communicate with your pendulum in a different manner, or if your pendulum wants to give you yes/no in a different manner, allow the energies to teach you how to use your pendulum.

mystic transformation

What is a mystic transformation? It is a radical transformation to our state of grace arising from the absence of fear, leading to our experiencing only joy from our heartfelt passions and pleasures. When we release guilt, shame, embarrassment, and feelings of greed, weakness, and selfishness, all stemming from conditional love and that we have associated with expressing our passion and pleasure, we release the negative circumstances that we have subconsciously created to "help" us repress the passion. In other words, when we experience "dis-ease", either internally or from a difficult situation external to us, there is always a spiritual root identifying a lack of self-acceptance and love.

Mystic Transformation lists negative circumstances and the associated spiritual state that requires opening in order to release the circumstance. For example, the affirmation associated with releasing procrastination is "I create faith in my future." Upon analysis, it is clear that if one has no faith in what the future holds, then one would extend his or her current circumstance as long as possible so as to remain in the perceived safety of the present. Faith in the future therefore erases the subconscious need to procrastinate.

Not all relationships between the ailment and the affirmation are clear, and understanding the relationship is not critical to healing. The magic of Mystic Transformation is that disease and struggle can be avoided before it manifests, or healed after it manifests, simply by using these affirmations to identify the aspect of repressed spirituality and then gaining the courage to express that aspect through the healing that **The Path to Heal** provides.

The list of ailments is divided into three categories: 1) physical symptoms 2) psychological / behavioral issues and 3) circumstantial situations. Please note that the categorization of symptoms into physical and psychological is not a scientific one; it has simply been broken down this way to make locating a symptom easier. The circumstantial category lists situations that are perceived as external to us, such as our phone not working or inclement weather. However, there are no situations that are truly external to us, as our energy, or communal energy, has created the negative circumstance.

This list does not include every negative circumstance that exists, as that would obviously be impossible. If you have a situation that is not on this list, a **Path** practitioner can gain insight into the Affirmation needed to transform your particular situation.

The list of Mystic Affirmations was channeled to me over the course of a long winter weekend filled with snow and ice storms. Its power was made clear to me while we waited out a long power outage from the storm. I received the affirmation for power outages: "I create sacred cosmic sense of order, rejuvenating my soul"; stated the affirmation using Divine Magic, and the power came back on within seconds. We lost power again for a lengthy period a few hours later. My daughter Anna received the affirmation for ice storms: "I create musical beauty". I did Divine Magic, and the power came back within a split second.

While simply recognizing the relationship between one's issue and the aspect of self that requires love and expression is an exciting first step to healing, the affirmations used in conjunction with **The Path to Heal** create mystical healing. When we incorporate Mystic Affirmations into Divine Magic, we not only gain physical healing, but we gain the courage to be unstoppable by infusing pure light into our passion and pleasure. This list can be used by anyone who has studied Divine Magic either by attending the half-day class or by teaching themselves using this manual. Each affirmation can be included in the Divine Magic daily practice to attract universal energies to help us overcome our fears and fully express self. If one is very blocked and is not able to transform through Divine Magic alone, then **Path** sessions will help uncover the story behind the wounding event at the root of the block and send much-needed healing energy to release this wound that we still carry.

Using Mystic Transformations in Divine Magic

- Mystic Transformation Affirmations are to be used as part of the Divine Magic daily practice.
- They are to be used to fill in the Divine Magic's "I create" statement.
- These affirmations are aligned with physical and situational conditions. Incorporate the relevant ones if they resonate with you.
- If there is more than one affirmation listed with a condition, incorporate as many as do resonate.
- Incorporate others that resonate even if you do not suffer from the corresponding condition.
- Feel free to dowse this list to identify affirmations to be included in your Divine Magic practice. *Note: If you dowse for an affirmation, it does not mean that you suffer from the negative circumstance or physical condition that corresponds to the affirmation.*
- If a loved one suffers from one of these conditions, the issue may mirror yours, and therefore the affirmation may be applicable to you as well.

∞ *I create _____ from my heart by honoring my divine, authentic and blissful self.* ∞

Condition	Mystic Affirmation

Condition	Mystic Affirmation
Physical	
AIDS	the empowerment of my identity
Allergies	
Food	affection for my basic needs
Dairy	the courage to succeed
Gluten	inspired joy
Seasonal	affection for my mystical true nature
Animals	infinite stillness
ALS	energetic peace
Alzheimers / Memory	infinite wisdom
Anal Fissures	powerful generosity
Ankle Pain	a blissful relationship with my infinite choices
Appendicitis	inner peace
Arthritis	adventure leading to success
Asthma	authentic relationships with loved ones
Back Pain	
General	deep affection for my emotions
Herniated Disc	mystical love
Bad Breath	easy laughter
Blood	
Anemia	peaceful inspiration
Aneurism	honest and intimate loving relationships
Clots	honesty
Low Blood Count	attractiveness
Low Platelet Count	caring assistance
Blood Pressure	
High	mindful living
Low	physical joy
Bones	
Broken	devotion to my spirited self
Spurs	joyful spirituality
Brain Damage	passionate contentment
Bursitis	youthful happiness

Condition	Mystic Affirmation
Cancer	
General	infinite love
Bladder	courageous expression of life
Breast	blissful relationship with other's admiration
Colon and Rectal	inspirational generosity
Endometrial	immunity to actions and opinions of others
Kidney	sensuality
Leukemia	forgiveness of life's burdens
Lung	breathing in my true spirit
Melanoma	loving kindness to self and others
Non-Hodgkin Lymphoma	generosity to self and others
Pancreatic	deep connection to God
Prostate	engagement with children
Thyroid	honest expression
Throat	loving kindness
Carpal Tunnel	spirited flexibility
Cellular Disorders	perfection
Cholesterol (high)	a blissful relationship with my diet
Chronic Fatigue	generosity to self
Concussion	joyful optimism
Congestion	liveliness
Cough	freedom of thought
Cracking Joints	infinite blessings
Cystic Fibrosis	the safe celebration of life
Diabetes	
General	a love of my sensuality
Hi Blood Sugar	attractive sensuality
Low Blood Sugar	energetic sensuality
Digestion issues	
General	conscious enlightenment
Blood in stools	the celebration of my truth
Constipation	sexuality
Diarrhea	nourishment from my gifts
Gas	dancing with bliss
Heartburn	passionate thought
Reflux	internal kindness
Down Syndrome	trust of human kindness
Ear Issues	enthusiastic laughter

∞ *I create* _____ *from my heart by honoring my divine, authentic and blissful self.* ∞

Condition	Mystic Affirmation
Elbow Pain	constructive and abundant life affirming work
Epilepsy	mystic healing
Epstein Barr Virus / Mono	energetic connection to the planet
Exercise	
Related Injuries	success
Resistance	spirited sexuality
Exhaustion	joyful spirituality
Eye	
General	the adoration of my spirit
Astigmatism	inspired stillness
Blindness	spirited contentment
Blurry	authentic joy
Cataracts	engagement with my talent
Detached Retina	gentle healing
Dry Eye	inspirational vision
Far-sighted	adventurous laughter
Focus	inspired peace
Glaucoma	spirited stillness
Heavy Eyelids	honoring my path to happiness
Near-sighted	easy living
Fainting	creative fluidity
Fever Sores	the love of laziness
Fibromyalgia	sensuality
Finger Pain	enjoyable work
Flu	generosity to my peaceful and loving ideals
Food Poisoning	deep affection for my God given wisdom
Foot	
General	my life's purpose
Bunions and Corns	acts of kindness
Pain	the courage to tell others what I need
Gall Bladder	generosity
Hair	
Grey Hair	my genius
Styling Issues	embracing chaos
Thinning/Loss	a warm and peaceful vocation
Head Cold	optimism
Headaches / Migraines	a blissful relationship with my mystical self
Hearing Issues	a love my inner wisdom

∞ *I create* _____ *from my heart by honoring my divine, authentic and blissful self.* ∞

Condition	Mystic Affirmation
Heart issues	
General	energetic generosity to self and others
Arterial Sclerosis	forgiveness of self
Irregular Heartbeat	an abundant perspective
Murmur	selfless love
Valve Issues	energetic fun
Hemorrhoid	sensuality and sexuality
Hepatitis	freedom from obligation
Hernia	powerful optimism
Hip Pain	a blissful relationship with what I know to be true
Inefficient	celebration of the future
Infections	infinite magic
Intestinal Issues	
Colitis and Crones	trusting my talents
IBS	consciousness
Cramps	relaxed relationship with pleasure
	sacred sexuality
Kidney	impassioned transformation
Knee Pain	a blissful relationship with life's adventure
Lyme Disease	conscious enlightenment
Meningitis	love's wisdom
Menopause	beauty
	a life without struggle
Menstruation Issues	
Cramping	relaxed creativity
Heavy Bleed	joyful maturation
PMS	awareness of my importance
	blissful relationship with my intellectualism
	love of my sensual and intimate nature
Movement (restricted)	honest joy
Multiple Sclerosis	mystical grace
	sacred sexuality
Muscle	
Cramps	flexibility
Spasm	tranquility
Strain	ingenuity
Weakness	laughter
Muscular Dystrophy	infinite grace

∞ *I create _____ from my heart by honoring my divine, authentic and blissful self.* ∞

Condition	Mystic Affirmation
Nail Issues	enthusiastic expression of my generous soul
Natural High (can't maintain)	powerful grace
Nausea	intellectual fun
Neck Pain	
General	celebration of my decisions
General	mystical awareness
Whip Lash	intimacy with spirituality
Nerves	
General	magical body enjoyment
Neuralgia	blissful relationship with being independent
Neuropathy	spreading my warmth
Organ Failure	
General	optimistic celebration of life
Heart	the joy of laziness
Lung	joyful creation of happiness
Liver	a loving spirit
Pain - Chronic	an artistic flow with my environment
	blissful relationship with my heart's desires
	presence
Parasites	a commitment to the truth
Parkinson's	relaxed connection to God
Plantar Fasciitis	standing up for what I know to be true
Pneumonia	an understanding of my body's needs
Pregnancy/Birth	
Breach	a rebirth of my mind, body and spirit
C Section	a life of ease
Excessive Labor	relaxed creation
Infertility	intimacy with my needs
Miscarriage	kindness to self
Nausea	self-love
Preeclampsia	trust
Premature Birth	life affirming faith
Prostate	healthy devotion to self
Sciatica	unstoppability
Sclerosis - Liver	peaceful mysticism
Scoliosis	creative celebration of my body
Seizures	graceful mystical pleasure
Self Esteem (Low)	the courage to know self

Condition	Mystic Affirmation
Sexuality:	
Dysfunction	magical joy
Lack of Expression	powerful artistic expression
	separation from my religion and/or community
Not Orgasmic	inspirational celebration
Shoulder Pain	weightlessness
Sinuses	
Pain	open mindedness
Sinusitis	authenticity
Skin issues	
General	sensual pleasure
Acne	blissful relationship with my sexuality
Rashes/Poison Ivy	contentment
Sleep	
Difficulty Sleeping	the empowerment of my spirit
Night Terrors	passionate thoughtfulness
Sleep Apnea	grace
Snoring	open generous forgiveness of my shadow
Stressful dreams	kind respect for my truths
Sore Throat	enthusiasm for expressing _____
STDs	grounded sensuality
Stomach	
Ache	Zen
Virus	mystical pleasure
Strep Throat	promotion of my talent
Sunburn	rejuvenation from the sun
Teeth	
General	infinite pleasure
General	delicious food being good for me
General	passionate orgasmic sexual creativity
Abscess	a joyful passionate life
Cavity / Root Canal	sugar making me look and feel good
Gum issues	fun
Wisdom Teeth	mystical musicality
Tendonitis	musicality
Testosterone (low)	spiritual love

Condition	Mystic Affirmation
Thyroid	
Hypo	devotion to my powerful expression
Hyper	boundaries
Tics	stillness
Toe Pain	a grounded free spirit
Tonsillitis	a charmed life
Tumors	
General	intimate connection with God
Cancerous	powerful and loving connection to self
Fatty	fun
Fibroid	creative companionship
Ulcer	brilliant light
Urination	
Continued Urge	faith
UTI	acceptance of the subtle truth
Varicose Veins	a blissful relationship with my free spirit
Viruses	a blissful relationship with my spiritual truths
Warts	playful transformation
Wrist Pain	inspired artistry
Yeast / Candida	intellectual grace

Psychological/Behavioral	Mystic Affirmation
Abandoned	positivity
Abused	forgiveness of self
Abusive	forgiveness of parents

∞ *I create* _____ *from my heart by honoring my divine, authentic and blissful self.* ∞

Condition	Mystic Affirmation
Addiction: 　General 　Alcohol 　Cell Phone 　Drugs 　Exercise 　Food 　Gambling 　Screens / Gaming 　Sex 　Smoking	 the celebration of my talented friendship with myself forgiveness of my unloving parent(s) expressive love success stillness emotional freedom powerful stillness abundant fun magic my joyful light
Aggression	compassion
Anger	unconditional self love
Annihilation	connection to my divine nature
Anxiety	pure light
Attention Deficit Disorder	courageous boundaries with outside stimulation
Autism Spectrum	a healthy ego
Bipolar Disorder	inspired passion
Blocked Healing 　General 　Healing Others	 constructive and abundant life affirming work pure joy from healing the world with my gifts faith in what I know to be true
Brain Fog	sensual boundaries
Bully	shining my light with conviction
Burdened	a blissful connection to my life's purpose
Clumsy	intentional transformation
Criminal Behavior	peace
Decision Overwhelm	awareness of the sacred cosmic sense of order
Defensiveness	my actualized self
Depression	pure joy
Destructive	inspiring my community
Direction (lack of)	blissful relationship with my personal power

∞ *I create* _____ *from my heart by honoring my divine, authentic and blissful self.* ∞

Condition	Mystic Affirmation
Disappointed	owning my heart's desires
Dishonesty	forgive a discouraging parent
Disorganized	the joy of an easy life
Disruptive	enjoyment of success
Dissociated Personality	generosity to my talented and lovely self
Egotistical	the celebration of my ideals, values and principles
Embarrassed	relaxed laughter
Exercise Related Injuries Resistance	 success spirited sexuality
Fighting	honesty
Greediness	enlightened spirituality
Hoarding	faith in the present moment
Homesickness	contentment
Hyper-vigilance	inspired stimulation
Hyperactive	acceptance of my spirited self
Inflexible	attunement to my divine rhythm
Insatiable	joy from my heart's desires
Insecurity	powerful self respect
Inspirational Block	spiritual adventure blissful relationship with my followers
Jealousy	abundant self-love
Learning Issues General ADD (specific to learning) Dyslexia Low IQ Processing Test Anxiety	 grace cherishing failure as a guidepost to success sacred cosmic sense of order divine actualization limitless solutions multidimensional thinking
Loneliness	an intimate relationship with my spirited goodness
Losing	blissfully sharing my gifts with the world

∞ *I create* _____ *from my heart by honoring my divine, authentic and blissful self.* ∞

Condition	Mystic Affirmation
Mid-life Crisis	happiness
Miracles (blocked)	from my words (abra cadabra – ancient Aramaic)
Movement (restricted)	honesty about what makes my heart sing
Muscle Testing Difficulty	being right
Narcissism	my twin flame
Obsessive Mind	playfulness
OCD	loyalty to my own principles
Overcommitted	relaxed prosperity
Overprotective	faith in our world
Overwhelm	passion that brings me pleasure the awareness that all decisions are good decisions
Panic Attacks	faith in my needs
Paranoia	honest acknowledgement of my needs
Perfectionism	passionate playtime
Pessimism	mystic transformation
Phobias	celebration of my open mindedness
Possessiveness	celebration of my wisdom
Procrastination	faith in my future
PTSD	an open mind
Sabotage	honoring my knowledge
Schizophrenia	inspired grace
Selfishness	a world of people who share their true colors
Shutdown	magic
Spacey/Scattered	an appetite for success
Stress	infinite pleasure

Trust
  Lack of Trust
  Untrustworthy
	
	magical passion
	optimism

∞ *I create* _____ *from my heart by honoring my divine, authentic and blissful self.* ∞

Condition	Mystic Affirmation

Ugly Behavior
  General
  Fascination With
	
	courageous artistry
	joyful relationships

Unpopular	a joyful relationship with my lovable self
Unpopular	infinite abundance
Unreliability	love of money
Villainize	clear conscious

Weight Issues:
  General
  General
  General
  Loss of Appetite
  Obesity
 	
  Overweight
 	
  Flab
  Too Thin
  Anorexia
  Bulimia
	
	a blissful relationship with my body
	food as joy
	body stillness
	enthusiastic celebration of life
	body enjoyment
	forgiveness of an unavailable parent
	fulfillment
	attractiveness
	the beautiful me
	passion
	pleasure
	the stimulation of my senses

Weird	passionate friendship with my true nature
Workaholic	joyful generosity to self

∞ *I create _____ from my heart by honoring my divine, authentic and blissful self.* ∞

Condition	Mystic Affirmation

Circumstantial	Mystic Affirmation
Animal Issues	
Aggressive with Animals	friendship
Aggressive with Humans	my powerful lively true spirit
Barks Too Much	friendship
Destructive	beautiful stuff
Fear of Strangers	love of people
Food obsessed	peaceful true spirit
Hyperactive	love of fun
Needy	friendship
Pet Sitting Issues	a love of fun
Runs away	adventure
Separation Anxiety	adventure
Urination/Defecation issues	spirited laughter
Appliances	
General	friendship with myself
Air Conditioner	emotional tranquility
Dish Washer	celebration
Dryer	energetic playtime
Heater	impassioned fire
Microwave	peaceful devotion
Oven / Stove	connection to universal experience
Refrigerator	joy
Washing Machine	relaxation
Astrological Energies	
Lack of Belief in Free Will	my own blissful reality
Retrograde Impacts	cosmic stillness
Business / Job	
Lack of Customers	impassioned promotion of my spiritual gifts
Stress	a warm and peaceful home
Undervalued	knowing self
Unemployed	feeling safe when I am important
Can't Catch a Break	a blissful relationship with my power

∞ *I create _____ from my heart by honoring my divine, authentic and blissful self.* ∞

Condition	Mystic Affirmation

Clothes
    Don't Fit
    Not Right
	
	infinite grace
	infinite expression of my power

Competition (too much)	blissful relationship with the passionate me

Contractors
    Did a Bad Job
    Too Pricey
    Unreliable
	
	the love of self expression
	artistry
	powerful play

Financial
    Devastation (real or fear of)
    Lack of Abundance
 	
    Worries
	
	shining my light upon the world
	mystical generosity
	invoking the infinite
	the blessings of my divine path

Food
    Don't Know What to eat
    Lack Of
	
	intimacy with self and family
	love of my family and community

Garden (overrun)	social stimulation
Homeless	safe love
Incarceration	encouraging others to be optimistic

Institutional
    Abuse of Power
    Breakdown
    Incompetence
    Red-tape
	
	abundance from love
	blessings from our power
	spirited playfulness
	prosperity

Investment (bad)	generous laughter
Legal Embroilment	playfulness
Mechanical Issues	transcendence of fear
Mold	loving supportive assistance
Pest Control	blissful relationship with our pleasure

∞ *I create* _____ *from my heart by honoring my divine, authentic and blissful self.* ∞

Condition	Mystic Affirmation
Planet Explosiveness	
Economic Unrest	loving respect
Epidemic	generous relaxation
Genocide	the understanding of my right to exist
Fire	inspirational fun
Human Rights Violation	faith in abundance
Infestation	open connection to God
Overpopulation	a love of nature
Persecution	learning
Pollution	abundant health
Poverty	thoughtfulness
Stock Market Unrest	generosity
Volcanic Eruption	mindful living
War	acts of kindness
Plumbing	fun
Power Outage	sacred cosmic sense of order rejuvenating my soul empowerment
Professionals	
Malpractice or Poor Service	extreme kindness to self
Too Pricey	joyful love
Property	
Isn't Selling	blissful relationship with change
Septic / Sewage Issues	a love of the forces of nature
Shortages	
Food	healthy generosity
Fuel	spiritual connection to the environment
Skyrocketing Prices	gratitude
Social Life / Romance	
Lack of / Uninspired	passion
Unreliable Friends	loveliness
Space	
Need to Fill	grace
Need to Empty	knowing that my future is easy
Not Enough	owning my heart's desires
Surgery	mystic transformation

∞ *I create* _____ *from my heart by honoring my divine, authentic and blissful self.* ∞

Condition	Mystic Affirmation
Technology Issues	
Cell Phone	peaceful communication with my loved ones
Computer	passionate and peaceful work
Email	a blissful relationship with success
Internet	universal experience
Printer/Scanner	inspired grace
Television:	
Nothing to Watch	joy with my loved ones
Remote Control Confusion	a fluid relationship with the new age
Time	
Not Enough to Do	faith in my presence
Too Much to Do	the joy of relaxation
Running Out	instantaneous transformation
Transportation	
Crashes	a clear passage
Delays/Jams	adventure
Mechanical Trouble	a carefree existence
	enjoyment of life
Weather	
Cancellations	peace, grace and joy
Drought	nourishment
Earthquake	energetic stillness
Extreme Cold	acts of kindness
Extreme Heat	friendship
Extreme Snow	energetic synchronicity
Flood	divine beauty
Global Warming	blissful relationship with my spirited nature
Hurricane	joy
Ice	musical beauty
Storm	mystic peace
	consciousness of oneness
Tornado	loving joy
Tsunami	healthy intimacy

Symbol	These techniques transmute energy allowing us to break patterns that are not serving us. Each technique has a different meaning defined below.	Chakra Diagram & Meaning
	Quantum Spin: Creates an alchemical reaction that opens the chakras to connect source to essence, the outcome of which is that we naturally align with our full potential. Quantum refers to a tiny input of energy creating a huge, immediate change.	
	Eyes Into Soul: Creates a window into our soul, so that we know our full potential.	
	Infinity Flower, or Heaven on Earth: The 3 interwoven infinities draw out the power of self-love to dissipate struggle.	
	Infinity: Invokes the infinite	
	Sublimation: Brings consciousness of our true nature by restoring us to our pure state and resolidifing our spirit and biochemistry to reflect that purity.	
	Spinal Adjustment or Alignment with God: Calms overactive reflexes that separate us from oneness (similar to a chiropractic adjustment).	
	I Am That I Am: This symbol amplifies our vibration so that we become fully conscious of, attract and have the faith to reach for that which brings us joy. It affirms our divinity, overriding negative thought patterns, leading to the manifestation of that which will bring us joy.	
	Tool: Spiral Wand – Divine Magic: continuous loop of unconditional love and light resonating our hearts to our mind so we can manifest our soul's purpose. This wand must have a spiral shape and include a rose quartz. The wand utilizes Abundance Harmonizer energy defined below.	1 - Grounding 2 - Sexuality/Creativity 3 - Personal Power 4 - Love 5 - Expression 6- Intuition 7 - Remembering God
	Abundance Harmonizer: (Archangel Michael) This harmonizer directs heart energy to the 1st and 7th Chakras to bring awareness to the illusion of scarcity. Once aware, all jealousy and fear dissipate and we relax in the sure knowledge that we receive abundance in all areas of life.	

Consciousness Harmonizer: (energy of Archangel Rafael) Harmonizes Good Health bringing us the experience of heaven on earth. We are in heaven on earth when we know absolute self-love, which by definition is the absence of guilt, shame and embarrassment. Without guilt, shame and embarrassment, all body systems are stabilized, regenerating our mind, body, spirit and soul.

Mystic Transformation: The energy from the symbol above gives us insight into our struggle and the sacred geometry of the overlaid ice crystal raises our vibration to that of pure light (which is the absence of fear), removing all guilt, shame and embarrassment from our heart-felt pleasure and passion.

Made in the USA
Middletown, DE
18 September 2015